What The Heck Is Happening With My Money?

Take Control of Your Finances: A Practical Guide for Every Individual

By

Arif Mohamed

Preface:

In today's rapidly c hanging financial landscape, understanding personal finance has become more important than ever. However, for many adults in India, the intricacies of managing money, investing wisely, and planning for the future remain elusive. This book, is a step in creating that gap by giving step-by-step, easily-digestible advice on how to take back control of your financial life.

Personal finance is not just about earning money—it's about managing it wisely to secure a comfortable and financially independent future. No matter you are beginning your career, planning to educate your kids, or preparing for retirement, learning the basics of personal finance will prepare you to make good choices at all stages of your life.

This book is designed to be a comprehensive yet accessible resource for Indian adults who want to build a strong financial foundation. I've crafted each chapter with the aim of simplifying complex financial concepts, from inflation and investments to insurance and budgeting, with a particular focus on how these topics relate to the Indian financial ecosystem. In addition to theoretical frameworks, you will also find practical tips, case studies, and concrete actions that you can implement to enhance your financial position.

In this book, in addition to learning how to make a profit from your investments by investing intelligently, you will also be taught the strategies to make your fortune last by applying the most appropriate insurance and risk management strategies. I will lead you through determining financial goals, assessing risk tolerance and developing a strategic financial roadmap consistent with your long-range goals. My hope is that by the end of this book, you will feel more confident in your financial decisions and empowered to take charge of your financial future.

Financial literacy is a journey, not a destination. It is a skill that develops gradually and that lifelong learning is essential. While reading this book, I would like you to have an open mind, a curious spirit, and use the ideas you learn in daily life. Because of the speed at which life moves these days, the sooner you get into the habit of managing your money wisely, the better off you will be in the long run.

Whether you are a beginner or someone with a basic understanding of finance, this book will serve as a practical guide, helping you to navigate the world of personal finance with confidence. Let's embark on this journey together, towards financial empowerment and security.

Sincerely,
Arif Mohamed

Introduction

In an era marked by rapid economic changes and an increasingly complex financial landscape, understanding the principles of personal finance has never been more important. However, for much of India's population making money management, intelligently making investment decisions, and planning for a secure future continues to pose daunting challenges. Despite the growing awareness about the need for financial literacy, many adults still find themselves ill-equipped to navigate the maze of financial products, tax laws, investment options, and insurance policies available in the Indian market. This book, aims to bridge that gap by offering a clear, comprehensive, and practical guide to understanding and managing personal finances.

The significance of financial literacy cannot be overstated. People also can be without the knowledge and the tools to become successful in managing finances, wealth and financial security. If it is also understood that it's not only about how to make money, then it is also imperative to know how to save money, how to invest it properly and how to guard it from possible risks. Financial literacy is about making informed decisions—whether it's choosing the right insurance, deciding between investment options, or understanding the impact of inflation on your savings. In short, it's the key to financial independence.

Money matters present special difficulties and special opportunities for Indian adults. The Indian financial landscape is large, comprising of both conventional and innovative financial tools for use as investment. Yet, it is also daunting to figure out and the multiple regulatory and economic forces that affect them. This book focuses on simplifying these complex topics, making them more relatable and actionable for anyone—whether you are a fresh graduate starting your career or someone nearing retirement and planning your future.

In the remaining chapters we will tackle these basic notions, namely, budgeting, debt reduction, and preparing for emergency. We also examine the fundamental investing topics, for example, stocks, mutual funds, corporate bonds, and so on. This book, on the other hand, gives special attention to the practical aspects, such as Systematic Investment Plans (SIPs), risk management, and goal-based investing, that can bring you to the financial success in the long run. Additionally, we'll examine the importance of insurance—both health and life—as well as the tools to protect your wealth from inflation and unforeseen circumstances.

Each chapter is designed to break down complex financial jargon into simple, understandable concepts. By focusing on the Indian context, this book will give you insights into the financial products and services that are most relevant to you. It will give practical examples and practical tips in computing that can be implemented as soon as possible in your own financial plan. Most importantly, it will inspire you to consider your financial destiny and take practical steps to ensure it.

Throughout this journey, we'll also discuss the emotional side of personal finance—how to handle market volatility, understand your risk tolerance, and make investment decisions that are in line with your long-term goals. Financial discipline is essential, and this bo ok will help you cultivate that discipline through consistent learning and informed decision-making.

Ultimately, Personal Finance Literacy for is not just about building wealth—it's about securing a life of peace and stability, free from financial stress and uncertainty. The sooner you start, the more you'll be able to benefit. Whether you're planning for a child's education, building your retirement fund, or just trying to improve your financial habits, the tools you need to succeed are right here.

I urge you do read this book with an open mind and challenge the exercises therein and actually try implementing the techniques that sit well with your way of thinking. Remember, financial literacy is an ongoing process where each step you take brings you closer to financial freedom.

By the end of this book, my hope is that you will have a deeper understanding of personal finance and feel confident in your ability to make sound financial decisions. Financial literacy is a journey that lasts a lifetime but, with appropriate information and way of life, could be even a journey that may open up various opportunities, a secure future and financial freedom.

Let's embark on this journey toward financial empowerment
and security together.

Sincerely,
Arif Mohamed

Table of Contents

Chapter1: Introduction to Personal Finance

Personal finance is the activity that involves structuring your budget involving everything you earn, save, buy, invest, and defend. It requires making sound financial decisions to achieve current and future security. In a rapidly changing financial landscape, understanding the basics of personal finance is essential for achieving financial independence and stability. Whether you are an employee, entrepreneur, or freelancer, personal finance applies to everyone, as the principles of managing money remain constant across different professions.

What is Personal Finance?

At its core, personal finance is about making smart financial choices that align with your life goals, whether that's owning a home, securing your retirement, or providing for your family. It includes a broad spectrum of financial endeavors and/or decisions that have personal implications, including:

Budgeting: Tracking income and expenses to ensure you live within your means.

Saving: Setting aside money for future needs and emergencies.

Investing: Disposition of funds to assets that can have a return over time.

Debt Management: Effective management of outstanding loans or credit card balances to prevent financial difficulty.

Risk Management: Protecting yourself from financial hardships through insurance or other financial safety nets.

All of these domains also have an important part to play in how you manage money and make financial decisions for the future.

Why Financial Literacy Matters

Financial literacy is the ability to understand and manage your finances effectively. It's about financial literacy, what to do with money, and how to stay out of financial trouble. With rising costs, inflation, and an unpredictable economy, it's more important than ever to have a solid understanding of personal finance. Without this knowledge, it's easy to make poor financial decisions, fall into debt, or miss opportunities to grow your wealth.

By increasing your financial literacy, you can:

Make informed decisions that positively impact your financial health.

Prevent over-spending, lack of saving, and under-investment mistakes.

Plan for future life goals and unforeseen financial emergencies.

Build wealth and achieve financial independence over time.

Key Concepts in Personal Finance

Mastering the basics of personal finance is the starting point for creating a sound financial future. Below are some core areas to grasp as you start your financial journey:

Income: It is the money that you make from multiple sources, for example, earning money from your job (salary), making money through your business or from passive incomes from real estate rentals or investments. Effective cash management includes, on the one hand, getting the maximum possible return and, on the other, using the obtained returns in the best possible way for savings, investments and expenses.

Expenses: Expenses are the costs you incur to live your life, such as rent or mortgage, utilities, groceries, education, and entertainment. It is important to monitor your spending, because it is through tracking spending that you will understand where your money is going, and in turn pinpoint places that you can reduce spending to save money.

Debt: Debt is borrowing money from creditors, usually in loan or credit card shape. While debt can be a useful tool for financing large purchases or investments (like a home or education), excessive or mismanaged debt can be detrimental to your financial health. The ability to manage and pay off debt is crucial to maintaining healthy finances.

Investments: Investments are financial instruments or property (i.e., stocks, bonds, and mutual funds) which enable to increase your funds in the long term. Investments may have a higher rate of return than deposit accounts and they expose the investor to higher risk. It is important to know various investment products and their relation to your financial aspirations.

Risk Management: Managing financial risk in the form of medical emergencies, loss of employment or other unforeseen circumstances is imperative. Insurance products such as life insurance, health insurance, and property insurance indemnify and protect so that you are not crushed by difficult financial surprises.

The Importance of Financial Planning

Financial planning is the activity of generating a map to reach your financial objectives. It is effective planning to establish very explicit targets, to assess your financial situation to start with, and come up with plans to achieve targets. Whether it's saving for retirement, buying a house, or paying off debt, financial planning ensures that you are moving in the right direction.

Key steps in financial planning include: Key steps in financial planning include:

Setting financial goals: Clearly define short-term and long-term financial goals.

Assessing your current financial situation: Understand your income, expenses, debts, and assets.

Creating a budget: Create a budget that allows you to achieve your targets all while handling your daily costs.

Investing for the future: Select an appropriate investment strategy given an individual's risk tolerance and time horizon.

Reviewing and adjusting: Continuously check your financial plan and modify this as your situations evolve.

The basis of the right personal finance is based on understanding of this principles. During the reading of this book, you will learn more and more about personal finance, from budget to investing and search for some strategies which could assist you to make the right financial decisions. The key takeaway is that with the right knowledge and planning, anyone can take control of their finances, minimize financial stress, and work towards building long-term wealth. Financial literacy is a lifelong journey, and mastering it will empower you to navigate the financial challenges of life and secure a prosperous future.

Chapter 2: Understanding Inflation

Inflation is one of the most relevant economic indicators determining everyone's financial status. It refers to the rate at which the general level of prices for goods and services rises over time, leading to a decline in the purchasing power of money. Essentially, inflation means that with the same amount of money, you can buy fewer goods and services than you could previously. Inflation is a major problem in India, because it has direct effect not only on cost of living, but also on the real value of savings and investments.

What is Inflation?

Inflation is the rise in prices of goods and services in an economy over time. It is usually assessed by the Consumer Price Index (CPI) or the Wholesale Price Index (WPI) of India, respectively. These indices relate to the price fluctuations of a particular group of goods and services frequently bought by households.

For example, if the inflation rate is 5% in a given year, it means that, on average, the prices of goods and services in the economy have increased by 5%. For example, if you had ₹1,000 at the beginning of the year, by the end of the year that ₹1,000 would buy you less and you would be limited to what ₹950 could buy you in the previous year.

How Inflation Affects Your Purchasing Power

The immediate consequence of inflation is it "eats away" at the value of your money. All of this changes with the increase of inflation, and the currency's value decreases, along with the prices of the daily necessities, that is food, fuel, housing and healthcare. This implies that, unless you are earning money at a rate that increases faster than inflation, you will lose money buying the same amount of stuff.

For example:

If inflation is 6%, a grocery bill of ₹100 will go up to ₹106.

Slowly over time it can take a heavy toll on people's household budgets just from price escalations.

Inflation can have both short-term and long-term effects. Short term you may experience an uptick in living costs. Over the longer term, inflation can seriously erode balances and investments so long as the balances and investments than they to account for the same level of real value.

Types of Inflation

Demand-Pull Inflation: This happens when supply of goods and services is insufficient to cover the demand, thus causing prices to rise. For example, if there is a boom in consumer spending or a government stimulus, the demand for goods and services increases, pushing prices up.

Cost-Push Inflation: This type of inflation occurs when the costs of production increase, leading businesses to raise their prices to maintain profit margins. For instance, an increase in raw material costs or labor expenses can result in higher prices for finished goods and services.

Built-in Inflation: This form of inflation is a consequence of past experiences (for example, workers who have been demanding to make up for higher living costs, hence each one has been requesting of businesses to increase price). It is also known as a wage-price spiral.

Impact of Inflation on Savings and Investments

Inflation will have major repercussions on both savings and investments:

Savings: Saving accounts, bond and fixed deposit FD) and low return investment products might not provide enough return to counter inflation. For instance, if you earn an interest rate of 5% on your savings and the inflation rate is 6%, your real return (after inflation) is negative. It follows that your money is depreciating even though it is in a "safe" investment.

Investments: Inflation can destroy the yield of investments, which may not be adjusted for inflation. For example, bonds, which offer fixed returns, may lose purchasing power over time. In the case of some investment products-for example, equities, gold and inflation-indexed bonds-the returns are widely thought to be a good inflation hedge as they tend to outperform inflation over time.

How Inflation Affects Different Financial Goals

Retirement Savings: In the long run, inflation can thereby greatly erode the purchasing power of investments in in the absence of exposure to inflation-protected securities. For example, if inflation is 6% annually and your retirement fund grows at a 4% return, the purchasing power of your savings will decrease over time.

Education and Home Buying: Inflation impacts large financial goals like education and buying a home as well. Costs of education and real estate are known to increase rates of inflation and is therefore crucial to invest early and judiciously in order to match these increasing expenses.

Insurance Premiums: The cost of insurance policies (health, life, etc.) Increases with inflation, so it is worthwhile updating your insurance regularly, just to make sure it covers future requirements.

Strategies to Protect Your Wealth from Inflation

Although inflation can be a nightmare, there are tactics you could take to reduce its impact and protect your wealth:

Invest in Equities (Stocks): Equities typically yield greater returns than the vast majority of other asset classes and have in the past consistently beaten inflation for the very long term. While equities come with volatility and risk, investing in a diversified portfolio of stocks can help protect your wealth from inflation.

Inflation-Linked Bonds: Government securities such as the Inflation-Indexed National Savings Securities (IINSS) are intended to insulate against inflation. The principal and interest rate of these bonds are periodically recalculated with reference to the index of primary products, with the objective to maintain the purchase value of your investment along with the increase of prices.

Real Estate: Property has traditionally been an excellent inflation hedge because property values have typically appreciated over time in tandem with or exceeding inflation. However, real estate carries associated risks, including illiquidity and market volatility.

Precious Metals (Gold): Whenever inflation, Gold is taken as a safe haven. Gold has a tendency to increase in price when inflation gets worse because it is seen as a safe haven. Investing in gold or gold-based investments, such as Gold ETFs, is one way to protect wealth during inflationary times. **Diversification:** An investment portfolio that is well-diversified and contains stocks, bonds, real estate and commodities could reduce the risk of inflation. Diversification spreads your risk and ensures that your wealth isn't entirely dependent on one type of asset.

Increase Your Income: One of the simplest ways to counter the effects of inflation is to ensure your income rises at a pace that matches or exceeds inflation. This may require negotiations on higher wages, seeking additional income sources, as well as learning new skills that lead to higher paying jobs.

Avoid Holding Too Much Cash: Because cash is losing its value with inflation, it is not safe to maintain big sums of money in savings accounts. Rather, place your money in assets that appreciate over time, to beat inflation.

Regularly Review Your Financial Plan: Inflation can alter the assumptions with which you made financial planning goals. Regularly review and adjust your financial plans to account for changes in inflation rates, income growth, and expenses.

Inflation is a fact of economic life, but with proper planning and approaches, you can offset its potential negative consequences for your financial future. Knowing how inflation drains the value of your money is crucial to making good money saving, investing, and cash management decisions. Through diversification of investments, inflation-linked bonds, and active work to enhance your income, these can effectively safeguard your assets and provide a safety net for your long-run financial objectives against the pressures of inflation.

Chapter 3: Investment Basics

Investing is one of the most powerful ways to grow your wealth and secure your financial future. When you channel funds into assets with the promise of a positive return, you gamify and turn your money into an active participant in market play. This chapter will delve into the importance of investing, explain the power of compound interest, and explore the different types of investments available in India, including equities, fixed income, real estate, and more.

What is Investing?

Fundamentally, investing is the process of placing your money into financial instruments i.e., stocks, bonds, mutual fund, real estate, or even business enterprises, with the aim of making income or generating capital appreciation (i.e., the asset value increases) that derives from investing. In contrast to saving, in which money is set aside for future use (usually at a low interest rate), investment engages risk-based strategies to potentially achieve a greater rate of return.

With investing, you can grow wealth over time, reach financial targets and win against inflation. It is a major ingredient in the accumulation of wealth over the long term, as it lets your cash earn more than is the simple interest on a savings account.

The Importance of Investing

Wealth Creation: Investing is the single most important step to wealth creation over the long run. Just saving money is not a guarantee for achieving financial goals as inflation depreciates the buying power of money. Investing allows us to realize returns over the long term, through compound growth, which can bring about remarkably high wealth growth.

Beating Inflation: Inflation depreciates the value of your money with the passage of time. Already have money in savings accounts with low interest, it is possible that this does not beat inflation. Investing in assets with better returns allows you to not only defend but also increase your assets at a rate greater than inflation.

Achieving Financial Goals: No matter if you purchase a house, pay for your child's schooling, or retire in style, investing is how you make your financial dreams come true. Following sound principles, investment can help you to reach these milestones financially.

Retirement Planning: Investing long term, you will be able to create a corpus that will provide you in retirement. Individuals relying on pensions, savings accounts, or government schemes on its own may fall short. Investments in the growth of equity, mutual funds and incomes can provide the growth that is required to continue your lifestyle in retirement.

The Power of Compound Interest

Compound interest is one of most potent ideas in investing. Compound interest is the interest earned not only on the principal amount itself, but also on the previously accumulated interest. This indicates that the value of your assets can increase by a factor of 2 over time, thus playing a significant role in wealth building.

Here's how compound interest works: Here's how compound interest works:

Assume that you deposit ₹1,000 at 8% interest per year. In the second year, you will get ₹80 (8% of ₹1,000).

In the second year, you will earn 8% on ₹1,080 (the original ₹1,000 plus the ₹80 interest earned in the first year). You will accrue ₹86.40 in interest for the second year.

For example, the cycle repeats, with the interest you earn growing every year.

The formula for compound interest is: The formula for compound interest is:

A= P(1+r/n)nt

Where: Where:

A = the capital gained from interest amount.

P = principal (the initial amount)

r = annual interest rate (decimal)

n = number of times interest is compounded per year.

t = time invested in rupees in years.

Although a small amount of cash invested on a regular basis, it continues to add up in substantial way thanks to compounding. That's why starting to invest early is essential for maximizing wealth creation.

Example: The Power of Compounding with Indian Investments

Let's say you invest **₹10,000** in a **mutual fund** that offers an annual return of **10%**, compounded yearly. You decide to leave the investment for **5 years** without withdrawing any money.

Here's how the investment grows year by year:

> **Year 1**: You start with ₹10,000. At the end of the year, you earn **10% of ₹10,000**, which is ₹1,000. Your total at the end of Year 1 is now **₹11,000**.

> **Year 2**: In Year 2, your total amount is now ₹11,000. At the end of the year, you earn **10% of ₹11,000**, which is ₹1,100. Your total at the end of Year 2 is **₹12,100**.

> **Year 3**: In Year 3, your total amount is now ₹12,100. You earn **10% of ₹12,100**, which is ₹1,210. Your total at the end of Year 3 is **₹13,310**.

Year 4: In Year 4, your total is ₹13,310. You earn **10% of ₹13,310**, which is ₹1,331. Your total at the end of Year 4 is **₹14,641**.

Year 5: Finally, in Year 5, your total is ₹14,641. You earn **10% of ₹14,641**, which is ₹1,464.10. Your total at the end of Year 5 is **₹16,105.10**.

Final Outcome:

After **5 years**, your ₹10,000 has grown to **₹16,105.10**.

Key Insight:

Notice how, each year, the interest amount increases because you're earning interest on both the original investment and the interest from previous years. This is the power of compounding where your money grows faster over time without you doing anything extra.

Types of Investments Available in India

India provides a wide variety of investment choices for investors, based on investors' risk tolerance, investment horizon and financial objectives. Now let us consider the most frequent types of investments:

Equities (Stocks)

Equities, or stocks, represent ownership in a company. As soon as you buy shares of a company, you own a part of the company. Stocks can yield very high returns, but with greater risk, since markets are very volatile.

Pros: Potential for high returns, dividends, and long-term capital gains.

Cons: Loss risk from market movement, is something that involves knowledge and research to select the best of stocks.

Investing in individual stocks or equity mutual funds (which pool money from many investors to invest in a diversified portfolio of stocks) can provide the opportunity for substantial growth over time.

Mutual Funds

A mutual fund is an investment pool of funds received from a number of investors, which are used to buy or sell assets, like stocks, bonds, or other asset classes. Mutual funds managed by professional fund managers can make diversification an accessible investment option for small investors.

Pros: Diversification, professional management, low investment required, easy for beginners.

Cons: Market volatility makes it a very high-risk investment in short term, returns are subject to market risk.

Mutual funds vary with respect to asset allocation, and the examples include equity mutual funds, debt mutual funds, and hybrid funds.

Fixed Income Investments (Bonds)

Bonds are debt investments where you give the government or the firm money, in exchange for payment of interest on the capital over a while and on the capital at maturity. Bonds are generally considered safer investments compared to stocks.

Pros: Steady income, lower risk than stocks, predictable returns.

Cons: Lower return than equities, has sensitivity to changes in interest rate.

In India, government bonds, corporate bonds, and municipal bonds are all very common. Fixed income option another is investing in Fixed Deposits (FDS).

Real Estate

Investing in real estate is the purchase of real estate, including residential property, commercial property, or land. Real estate, due to its potential to generate income (e.g., through rental properties) and capitalization, is regularly viewed as a low-risk, long-term investment.

Pros: Tangible asset, rental income potential, potential for appreciation, portfolio diversification.

Cons: High upfront capital, illiquidity, market volatility, maintenance costs.

Real estate investment can be made directly or by way of real estate investment trusts (REITs), which is a less expensive means of investing directly in real estate without owning physical real estate.

Gold and Precious Metals

Gold has warranties of being a safe haven asset in the context of an inflationary or economically unstable era. An investment in physical forms (jewelry, coins) or in financial vehicles (Gold ETFs or Sovereign Gold Bonds (SGBs) can be made for gold.

Pros: Hedge against inflation, easily bought and sold, relatively liquid.

Cons: No income (no dividends or interest), variant price volatility.

Alternative Investments

Alternative investments are non-traditional investment options, which may include:

Cryptocurrencies: Digital currencies like Bitcoin and Ethereum. Cryptos are highly volatile and speculative.

Peer-to-Peer (P2P) Lending: Money lending directly to borrowers via online platforms connecting lenders and borrowers. It can offer high returns but carries higher risk.

Venture Capital: Investing in early-stage companies or startups. Although it may bring enormous gains, it is very risky.

These are generally associated with a higher level of risk, but have potentially greater returns than conventional investments.

Risk and Return

Every investment carries some level of risk. The general principle is that higher risk comes with the potential for higher returns, while lower-risk investments tend to offer lower returns. Understanding your risk tolerance (the level of risk you are comfortable taking) is essential in determining the right mix of investments for your portfolio.

Low Risk: Government bonds, Fixed Deposits, blue-chip stocks.

Medium Risk: Mutual funds, real estate, corporate bonds.

High Risk: Individual stocks, cryptocurrencies, P2P lending.

An optimized risk-exposure portfolio spreads investments across asset classes, reducing risk while maximizing the opportunity for return.

Investments play a significant role in personal Finance, through the growth of wealth, realization of the financial goals and protection against inflation. No matter if you are just starting or looking for ways to diversify, learning about the different places to invest in India will save you from making the wrong choices. If you make it possible to understand the nature of risk and return, compound growth and the behavior of various classes of assets, you can construct a diversified investment plan tailored to your financial objectives and risk profile.

Chapter 4: Investment in Mutual Funds and SIP

Mutual funds and Systematic Investment Plans (SIPs) are popular and accessible investment options that allow individuals to grow their wealth over time with professional management and diversification. In this subsection, we shall discuss the concept behind mutual funds, the idea of SIPs, the advantages of mutual funds, including rupee cost averaging, and compounding of returns.

What are Mutual Funds?

Mutual fund is a financial instrument that gathers money from many investors to invest in a diversified basket of assets, including stocks, bonds, money market instruments, or more than one of the above. The consolidated money is managed by a professionally operated fund manager who takes all the investment decisions according to the objective of the fund.

Mutual funds are a variety of mutual funds according to the investment proposition, in the below sense:

Equity Funds: Holds an investment focus predominantly in stocks, i.e., equities, and is suitable for high-risk investors who are seeking long-term capital gains.

Debt Funds: They hold fixed-income exposures, for example government bonds, corporate bonds, and treasury bills. They are, relatively speaking, safer and provide a fairly stable income along with relatively modest returns as compared to equity funds.

Hybrid Funds: These are the hybrid of equity investments and debt investments, a balanced risk-return mix.

Index Funds: These funds track the performance of a market index (like Nifty 50 or Sensex).

Sectoral Funds: These are concerned with particular fields such as technology, health, or energy, whereby investors can focus on particular industries.

By investing in a mutual fund, you purchase units of the fund, and the price of those units depends on the price of the underlying assets. The value of the commodity of one unit is called the Net Asset Value (NAV) which changes daily according to the returns of the fund's investments.

Benefits of Investing in Mutual Funds

Diversification: Diversification is, of course, a main advantage of mutual funds. Instead of money on a single security, mutual funds pool the money for many securities, eliminating the risk that a single investment would have a negative effect on the entire portfolio. This diversification helps mitigate risks and smoothen returns.

Professional Management: Mutual funds are managed by professional fund managers, who are experts in the markets of finance. They study the market, research companies, and make investment decisions on your behalf. It saves you time and energy, and it guarantees proper management of your investments.

Liquidity: Mutual funds are, in a way, more liquid in nature than real estate and fixed deposits. Investors can redeem their mutual fund units at the current NAV, making it a flexible investment option. Still, the liquidity is targetable by fund type (e.g., equity funds may be more difficult to liquidate than liquid funds).

Affordability: Mutual funds enable investors to invest with relatively modest capital, since they are not necessarily limited by the need to amass huge amounts of capital to start investing. Because of this exploitation, they are available to small and large investors.

Regulation: In India, mutual funds are controlled by the Securities and Exchange Board of India (SEBI) with transparency, responsible investor protection, and compliance with the best practices of the industry. The SEC's scrutiny bolsters the mutual fund investment process.

What is a Systematic Investment Plan (SIP)?

A Systematic Investment Plan (SIP) is a disciplined way to invest in mutual funds, where an investor commits to investing a fixed amount of money at regular intervals (monthly, quarterly, etc. SIPs enable you to invest in mutual funds without the risk of market timing. Using SIP, it is possible to start investing at as little as ₹500 per month, which is a very low-cost option for a large number of investors.

Here's how SIP works: Here's how SIP works:

You choose a mutual fund scheme.

You fix the amount of investment that you plan to make periodically (e.g., ₹2,000 per month).
The amount is automatically separated from your bank account and transferred to your mutual fund of selection.

The mutual fund units are purchased at Net Asset Value (NAV) current at the time of the investment.

Benefits of SIPs

Rupee Cost Averaging: A major benefit of SIPs is rupee cost averaging. This means that when you invest a fixed amount regularly, you end up buying more units when the market is down (when prices are lower) and fewer units when the market is up (when prices are higher). This smooths the overall cost of your investment and mitigates the effect of short-term market fluctuations.

For example: For example:

In January, if the NAV of a mutual fund is ₹100, you can buy 10 units for ₹1,000.

In February, if the NAV drops to ₹80, one can repurchase 12.5 units for ₹1,000.

As time goes by, your unit cost will decrease on average, and your capital is protected against market movements without having to time the market.

Compounding Returns: SIPs enable you to take advantage of the power of compounding. If you reinvest your earnings (i.e., dividends, capital gains), your investment will increase exponentially with time. The more time you have to be invested, the more equity your money earns. This is one of the most fundamental reasons why it is best to bring an SIP as early as possible, so that the capital it could amass in the long run is large.

For instance, if ₹5000 is invested every month into an SIP with an average annual return of 12%, the corpus can accumulate substantially over 10, 20, or 30 years, due to the force of compounding.

Discipline and Consistency: SIPs encourage disciplined investing. By setting up an automatic deduction from your bank account, you ensure that you stay committed to your financial goals. This consistency helps you stay on track and avoid impulsive spending or market timing.

Affordability: SIPs are relatively low cost as one can begin investing with relatively small amounts of money for most people. You don't need a big upfront lump sum to get started with mutual fund investment. Whether you can afford ₹500 or ₹50,000 per month, SIPs can accommodate different levels of financial capacity.

Flexibility: SIPs are flexible. The amount you invest, the duration of your investment, and the mutual fund scheme you are using can be changed at any time at any stage of your investment depending on your financial circumstance or your investment objective. This elasticity Enables you to tailor your investments to your growth.

Risk Mitigation: Through the continuous investment, SIPs smooth out the market's ups and downs, thus alleviating the risk of making wrong investment at the wrong time. Even though markets fluctuate, SIPs help reduce the emotional aspect of investing and prevent investors from making hasty decisions based on short-term market movements.
How to Choose the Right Mutual Fund for SIP?

While choosing a mutual fund for an SIP investment, keep the following factors in view:

Investment Objective: Select a mutual fund that is consistent with your financial ambitions. Are you seeking long-term growth (equity funds), short-term income (debt funds) or a mix of both (hybrid funds)?

Risk Tolerance: Consider your risk appetite. If you are young and have a higher risk tolerance, you can invest in equity funds. Debt/hybrid funds may be preferred by those who are nearing retirement or have low risk appetite.

Past Performance: Although past performance does not guarantee future returns, analysis of a fund's historical performance can give you some idea of its behavior under various market environments. Look for consistency over the long term.

Expense Ratio: The expense ratio is the cost that the fund house imposes for managing the mutual fund. Less of the fund's returns are deducted from itself, so when the expense ratio is lower it means more of your returns are given back to you. Search for that won't charge a high expense ratio to help your investment outperform.

Fund Manager's Expertise: The track record of mutual fund performance is frequently affected by the skills of the fund manager. Research the experience and track record of the fund manager before making your decision.

Mutual funds and SIPs are a good option for anyone to accumulate wealth on a long-term basis, whatever their financial status. Through the sharing of pool resources with other investors, mutual funds give access to diversified portfolios and professionally managed. Especially the SIPs are a simple and disciplined technology to make regular investments and accumulate the advantage of the rupee cost averaging and compounding returns. Regardless if you are a newbie or an advanced investor mutual funds and SIP can be fundamental to your long-term financial plan and can help you reach your financial goal in a consistent and simple way.

Chapter 5: Corporate Bonds as an Investment Option

Corporate bonds are a widely used type of investment wherein investors can lend money to companies, and receive interest payments periodically and principal amount at the maturity of the bond. They are fixed-income securities - i.e., they are known to return a certain amount of interest payments.

How Corporate Bonds Work

When a firm wants to borrow money to expand, operate, etc., it may borrow by issuing bonds rather than borrowing money from banks or issuing additional equity. When investors buy corporate bonds, they're essentially making a loan to the company. As security, the company agrees to pay the investor a fixed rate of interest (the coupon rate) for a given period of time. At the end of this period, when the bond reaches its maturity, the company will repay the principal amount (also called the face value or par value) of the bond.

Bonds vs. Equity Investments

Corporate bonds and stocks (equity investments) are both vehicles to invest in a company, however, in different ways:

Bonds represent debt: As a bondholder you are a creditor of the company and your main goal is to obtain regular coupon payments and at maturity the principal amount. Bondholders are typically repaid before equity shareholders in the event of bankruptcy.

Equity investments represent ownership: Shareholders own a stake in the company and their returns are directly tied to the company's profit and the stock price. Equity holders may receive dividends, but their returns are generally more variable than bond coupon interest.

The key differences are:

Risk: Bonds are regarded a lower risk than stocks, because interest payments are fixed while stock values can vary and dividends may not be paid.

Returns: Bond returns are typically more stable but often lower than equity returns. At the same time, when market conditions are unstable bonds can show the qualities of a powerhouse.

Seniority in claims: Bondholders get paid in liquidation before equity holders.

Risks and Rewards of Corporate Bonds

Risks:

Credit Risk: If the company gets into financial trouble, defaults, or otherwise is unable to make interest payments or principal payments, bondholders will be left with a loss. The risk of default must be taken into account when determining the creditworthiness of the company.

Interest Rate Risk: Increased interest rates can reduce the market value of outstanding bonds, as new bonds bearing higher interest rates are issued and the outstanding ones become less desirable.

Inflation Risk: As the inflation rises, the real value of both interest payments and principal of the bond may fall.

Liquidity Risk: It may be hard to sell corporate bonds before maturity if no adequate market for the bonds is available.

Rewards:

Stable Income: Corporate bonds offer recurring coupons, which makes it an interesting security for income investors.

Predictability: Bonds offer predictable returns, particularly if held to maturity, making them easier to plan for compared to the volatility of stocks.

Diversification: Investment portfolios can gain diversification from the risk inherent in equities through the use of corporate bonds.

Capital Preservation: Conservatively-minded investors bonds and so on come with the relatively secure (especially high-rated) backing of major institutional investors with deep pockets and the equity of well-known companies.

Assessing the Credit Rating of Companies

The credit rating of an enterprise is one of the critical parameters for bond assessment. Credit rating agencies (e.g., Crisil) assign a company's creditworthiness in fulfilling its debt obligations. These ratings go from investments (corresponding to higher risk of default) admissions to junk/high-yield bonds (corresponding to higher risk).

Investment-grade bonds (e.g., rating of AAA to BBB) are issued by well-managed, financially solid corporations with diminished default risk.

High-yield (junk) bonds (bonds rated below BBB) are issued by companies with less than stellar financial results, therefore they are riskier investments. By providing higher interest rates to reflect this risk, they.

A credit rating of a company plays a critical role in setting the yield on its bonds. More ratings correspond, in general, to lower yields and less ratings correspond to higher cultivated yields because the rates of return are lower for more sensitive metrics.

Evaluating Corporate Bonds in the Context of Your Financial Goals

It is crucial to take financial goals, risk appetite and time horizon into considering for corporate bond valuations in the following:

Income Needs: If you're seeking regular income, bonds with higher yields may be appealing. However, higher yields usually come with increased risk.

Risk Tolerance: For those who like to play it safe in investments, investment-grade bonds are a safer option. On the other hand, if you're comfortable with more risk in exchange for potentially higher returns, high-yield bonds might be a good fit.

Time Horizon: Duration of the bond that you intend to maintain matters. When you hold it until maturity, price variations related to interest rate changes or credit downgrades may be less important, but if you expect to sell before maturity, this aspect is more critical.

Corporate bonds are a useful means of income investors and they can provide reasonably stable income relative to equities. They always bring risks, particularly to credit quality, rates of interest, and inflation, but when they are carefully chosen, they can deliver steady income and diversification in an investment portfolio. Assessing credit rating of a company and taking into account your financial targets will provide direction to your investment decisions.

Chapter 6: Understanding Term Insurance

Term insurance is a form of life insurance that provides financial security to your family members after your death due to unexpected/abnormal death. It is one of the easiest and cheapest life insurance products, with qualification for a very high sum assured at a fairly low premium. The policy is designed to pay out a death benefit to your beneficiaries, in case you die during the policy period, which usually lasts 10 to 30 years. In contrast to other types of life insurance, term insurance does not generate cash value, or other investment benefits and is essentially a financial safety net for surviving family.

Benefits of Term Insurance

Affordability: Term insurance is one of the cheapest types of life insurance. The premiums are generally lower compared to permanent life insurance policies like whole life or universal life insurance, making it accessible for individuals seeking affordable coverage.

High Coverage Amount: Term insurance provides you with the opportunity to guarantee a big sum assured (death benefit) [i.e, for drawing a demise from which your (heirs or dependents may be drawing) received by your beneficiary(es) in the event of your own death. This is particularly useful if you are dependent on, on loan for, or obligated for substantial financial responsibility other than money.

Simplicity: The policy is quite simple, in that it has a simple format of making periodic payments (premiums) to the insurer and the insurer has a guarantee of paying your beneficiaries the sum assured to them in case of your death within the policy period.

Flexibility in Policy Terms: Term insurance policies usually offer freedom in the scope of coverage period, from short term (10-20 years) to long term (30 years or more) terms depending on the needs and financial targets.

Tax Benefits: In several nations, the premiums paid for terms life insurance policies are allowed for tax deductions based on the applicable provisions of income tax statutes (e.g., in India, Section 80C). Furthermore, the death benefit paid to your beneficiaries is typically tax-free.

No Cash Value: Although, some individuals may perceive this as a drawback, the absence of a cash value/investment element in term insurance may, in reality, result in still lower premiums. In contrast to whole life policies that merge insurance with a savings or investment stream, term insurance only addresses the issue of ex ante financial security.

Riders and Add-ons: Numerous insurers provide riders (attachments) to term insurance policies, e.g., in the form of critical illness, accidental death benefit or waiver of premium. These add-ons extend the coverage provided by the standard policy.

How to Choose the Right Term Insurance Policy

Selecting an appropriate term insurance policy is based on your personal financial status, family requirement, and future aspiration. Here are some important factors to consider:

Sum Assured:

The sum assured (death benefit) must be as large as possible to at least provide your family with sufficient living expenses, cover existing debts (e.g., mortgage or personal debt), and accommodate future obligations (e.g., children's education or marriage). Financial specialists typically suggest that your coverage should be between 10-15 times of your annual salary.

Think about the future requirements of your family and the issue of inflation when setting the right sum assured.

Policy Term:

The period of the policy is, ideally, applicable to your financial obligations. Insurance for instance, if you are raising kids, for example, you can choose to buy a long-term (relatively) insurance policy so that their access to education and overall wellbeing are secure, even if you pass away.

A policy term until your retirement age (say 60 or 65) may also be a good option if your financial obligations taper off with time.

Premiums:

The price of the premium has to be within the range of your budget but still provide enough protection. Although term insurance is relatively inexpensive premiums, make sure that the policy that you select is not draining your finances.

There is also an option of standard premium plan or premium plan with restricted premium payment period in which the premium is paid for a lesser time but the coverage for a longer time.

Riders and Add-ons:

Compare the riders/add-ons and make a suitable policy to meet your specific needs. For instance, adding a critical illness rider can provide a lump sum payout if you're diagnosed with a critical illness like cancer or heart disease, offering added financial protection.

Check for the availability of accidental death and disability riders as well.

Claim Settlement Ratio:

There is benefit in selecting an insurer that has a good claim settlement history. Claim settlement ratio measures how well an insurance company processes its claims. A higher ratio typically means a more reliable company.

Company Reputation:

Investigate reputation, financial soundness and customer service of the insurance company. A reputable company having robust financial backing is in a better position to pay in the future.

Review and Adjust as Needed:

Your insurance requirements may also vary over time, depending upon changes in your personal financial status, family situation or life stage. Be sure to periodically review your policy and adjust the coverage amount or policy term as necessary.

When Should You Buy Term Insurance?

Young and Healthy: The earlier you purchase term insurance, the lower the premiums you will pay. Insurers tend to provide lower premiums to young and healthy people.

Growing Family: Purchases of term insurance can also provide financial safeguard for dependents, including spouse, children, or elderly parents, in the event of your death.

Debt Obligations: If you have significant debts, like a home mortgage or business loans, term insurance can ensure that these debts are cleared without burdening your family.

Long-term Financial Planning: But to take care of your future needs and provide for your beneficiaries when no longer around, purchasing term insurance as part of an overall long-term financial plan can be a wise choice.

Term life insurance is a practical and cheap life insurance scheme that will guarantee financial security of your family in case of your death. Its ease of use, low cost and wide coverage make it often of choice to most people. By assessing your financial needs, understanding the policy terms, and choosing a reliable insurer, you can select the right term insurance policy that provides peace of mind for you and your loved ones.

Chapter 7: Health Insurance: Protecting Yourself and Your Family

Health insurance is an essential financial tool that provides coverage for medical expenses, ensuring that you and your family are protected from the high costs of healthcare. It can also reduce the financial strain of medical treatment, hospitalization, surgery, doctor visits, and all other health care. In this chapter, we'll explore the importance of having health insurance, the different types of health insurance plans available in India, and the key factors to consider when choosing a health insurance provider.

Importance of Health Insurance

Financial Protection Against Medical Expenses:

Healthcare is expensive, and without insurance you may be powerless to access the necessary care, particularly for serious illnesses or accidents. Health insurance offers financial security by covering a significant portion of medical costs which can prevent out-of-pocket costs that can deplete savings.

Access to Quality Healthcare:

Health insurance provides access to a wide network of hospitals and medical professionals. Most policies also provide cashless facility in network hospitals i.e., You don't need to pay the treatment fee upfront, as the insurance company will directly pay the bill with the hospital.

Coverage for Unforeseen Medical Events:

Medical emergencies, accidents, or sudden illnesses are unpredictable. Healthcare insurance helps to prepare you financially for such unforeseen health events, and brings peace of mind for both personally and your family.

Preventive Care and Health Check-ups:

A lot of health insurance policies are designed for prevention and coverable routine health check-ups, vaccination and screenings, o. These advantages can also be utilized for the early diagnosis of possible health issues with subsequent timely treatment and improved results.

Tax Benefits:

In India, health insurance policy premium is eligible for tax deduction under the provisions of Section 80D of the Income Tax Act. This provides an additional incentive to purchase health insurance, as it reduces your overall tax liability.

Cumulative Benefits:

Certain policies provide a No-Claim Bonus (NCB), which is a benefit that either bumps your sum insured higher in each policy year or reduces your premium amount for the year when no claims are filed. This can significantly benefit long-term policyholders.

Types of Health Insurance Plans in India

There are various kinds of health insurance schemes in India, each meant for diverse purposes and the needs of persons. The key types include:

Individual Health Insurance:
This type of plan covers only the individual policyholder. It is ideal for those who want to insure themselves against medical costs, especially if they have few dependents. The sum insured is, in general, selected according to personal requirements and medical conditions.

Family Floater Health Insurance:
It is a family floater plan that extends the cover among the whole family on a single policy. In it, there is an aggregated sum insured which can be spread among the family members. This kind of plan is cost-efficient for families, as the premium is usually less than buying her/his own policies for each family member.

Critical Illness Insurance:
This policy applies to life-threatening illness (e.g., cancer, myocardial infarction, renal failure, and so on). If diagnosed with a critical illness, the policy pays a lump sum amount, which can help cover treatment costs. This plan can be added as a rider to an existing health insurance policy or purchased separately.

Top-up Plans:
Top-up health plans provide additional health protection on top of your current health insurance scheme. These plans are

useful if you have a basic health insurance plan, but are requiring supplemental coverage to cover higher medical costs. Top-up plans generally come with a higher deductible (the amount you pay out of pocket before the insurer covers the costs).

Personal Accident Insurance:

Personal accident policies provide indemnification in the event of an accidental death, disability or being hospitalized due to an accident. Such policies are usually cheap and offer the extra coverage in case of accidents.

Maternity Health Insurance:
Maternity health insurance provides coverage for expenses related to pregnancy, childbirth, and post-delivery care. Plans may also include newborn care during the first months postpartum.

Hospital Cash Plans:
These plans assure a certain amount per day as a daily benefit, for each day spent in the hospital, even if the real costs aren't. They can have effects on non-medical costs such as transport, and after-discharge expenses.

Senior Citizen Health Plans:
These plans are tailored to people 60 and older. They offer coverage for age-related health issues, including hospitalization, surgeries, and critical illness treatments. In general, premiums are more expensive for older adults who have greater health risks as they age.

Factors to Consider When Choosing a Health Insurance Provider

Selecting an adequate health insurance plan is one of the important factors in guaranteeing the appropriate selection of medical services by individuals under health insurance. Following are some important factors to take into account when choosing a health insurance company.

Coverage and Inclusions:
That the policy should provide for an exhaustive type of medical expenditure, covering hospitalization, operatively surgery, daycare, pr As far as cerebellar-related emotions are concerned, atypical personal wiring could involve regions other than the vermis, leading to emotions triggered by local signals within extended networks. In addition, verify whether the policy includes coverage of critical illness, maternity, and other special requirements.

Network Hospitals:
Select an insurance with a very extensive network of hospitals especially in your region or locations where you may be required medical attention. Network hospitalization cashless services are one of the important advantages to streamline the reimbursement process.

Premiums and Affordability:
Estimate the premiums in terms of your wallet and, iteratively, plans from various insurers. Although ensuring adequate coverage is prioritised, premiums should be fair and maintainable over the long term.

Claim Settlement Ratio:

The claim settlement ratio is the measure of a level at which an insurance company effectively settles its claims. A larger ratio signifies that one tends to settle claims more quickly. This is a relevant aspect on which to focus so as to avoid any delays in the management of your claims.

Waiting Periods:

Health insurance policies come with certain waiting periods before specific benefits can be claimed. For example, coverage for critical illness might have an initial waiting period of 30 days to 90 days. Ensure that the policy terms align with your needs and that the waiting periods are not overly long.

Sub-Limits and Co-payments:

Certain forms of treatment have sub-limits allowed, such as room rent, ICU charges, or surgery charges, by some of the policies. Review these limits carefully to ensure they don't restrict your coverage. Co-payment clauses involve you paying part of the cost of medical treatment, so make sure this applies to the plan.

Renewability and Lifetime Coverage:

Make sure that the policy offers lifetime renewability and does not impose any age limit for renewal. As you age, your health risks increase, and a lifetime renewal guarantee ensures that your coverage continues as long as you need it.

Exclusions:
Carefully read the policy exclusions to be informed of all things regulated out of the policy scope. Standard exclusions are treatment for antecedent disorders (during initial waiting period), plastic surgery, and some of the lifestyle disorders.

Customer Support and Service:
Choose an insurance company known for its strong customer support and service. Effective support will give you the ability to track claims and to understand policy coverage.

Health insurance is an essential tool for safeguarding yourself and your family against the high costs of medical treatment. It is possible to have the financial security to weather health crises through the proper health insurance policy. All the kinds of plans that are available in India are understood and based on the criteria of coverage, affordability, network of hospitals, and claim settlement record, one can choose wisely which can answer the health requirements and give him/her future comfort.

Chapter 8: Building and Maintaining an Emergency Fund

An emergency fund is a financial safety net which can cover unforeseen situations or financial upheavals, e.g., medical emergencies, car damage, unemployment or urgent home maintenance. A financial emergency fund guarantees you will not have to use credit cards, loans or borrow money from family and friends in situations of financial crisis. In this chapter, we'll explore the purpose of an emergency fund, how much you should save, and the best investment options to ensure liquidity and safety for your emergency fund.

Purpose of an Emergency Fund

Financial Security:

The primary purpose of an emergency fund is to provide financial security during unexpected events. Life is lived in situations of the unforeseeable, such as when a medical emergency occurs, a car stalls, or one suddenly loses a job, and these things leave a financial burden. An emergency fund is there to help you weather these situations without incurring debt or jeopardizing your financial wellbeing.

Avoiding Debt:

In the absence of emergency fund, individuals often get themselves into credit card or loan debt for unexpected costs. This may result in the accrual of debt that, as a result, becomes hard to control in the context of the high-interest rates. With a specifically accumulated emergency fund, you will not be caught in a debt spiral in times of strife.

Peace of Mind:

If you are aware that you have financial reserves, it will help lessen the stress and increase the sense of control over your finances. It enables you to concentrate on the making of the solution rather than on the cost of it.

Financial Flexibility:

An emergency fund gives you flexibility to make important decisions without being financially cornered. For example, if you lose your job, your emergency fund can cover living expenses while you search for a new job. This also decreases the pressure to take any job just to survive.

How Much Should You Save in Your Emergency Fund?

How much you should save in your emergency fund depends on many things such as lifestyle, spending, and financial commitment. However, a general rule of thumb is:

3 to 6 Months of Living Expenses:

Financial experts generally advise having savings equivalent to 3 to 6 months of living expenses. This level of cash gives an acceptable buffer to withstand most crises, like unemployment, any serious medical bill. It will have to include the cost of essentials such as rent, utility, food, insurance and transportation.

Assessing Your Personal Situation:

i. Single or Dual Income Household: If you are the sole breadwinner or if you live in a single-income household, you may want to aim for a larger emergency fund (closer to 6 months of expenses) to ensure you have a buffer in case of job loss or other setbacks.

ii. Dependents: If you have dependents, such as children or elderly parents, you may need to save more to cover their needs as well.

iii. Job Stability: In jobs or industries that are volatile (e.g., freelance, contract-based employment), there may be a desire to accumulate more savings for the possibility of income gaps.

iv. Existing Debts: If you have significant existing debt, it may be wise to prioritize paying down some of that debt before fully focusing on building your emergency fund.

Start Small and Build Gradually:

If saving 3 to 6 months of expenses feels too much pressure, begin small and build your way up to your goal. Set a target of 1 month of expenses as a baseline and then incrementally increase it with each rise in income and savings.

Best Investment Options for Your Emergency Fund

In the context of forming an emergency fund, liquidity and safety are crucial. You want your funds to be easily accessible when needed, and you don't want to risk losing any money due to market fluctuations. The most appropriate investments for your emergency fund are low-risk and easily liquid. Some options include:

Savings Account:

A savings account is one of the simplest and safest methods for your emergency fund. It provides convenient access to your money and is guaranteed by the government up to a certain amount (for instance, ₹5 lakh in India with the Deposit Insurance and Credit Guarantee Corporation, or DICGC). Although interest rate on savings account is in a general low level, your fund is protected and liquid.

Fixed Deposits (FDs):

Fixed deposits are also a safe possibility for your emergency fund. FDs provide a stable interest rate for a defined time and are thus a low-risk product. On the other hand, the downside is that you have to "lock up" your funds for a while and penalties can arise if you withdraw the funds early. For an emergency fund, opt for a liquid FD or one with a short maturity period (3-6 months), which allows easier access to funds in case of an emergency.

Liquid Mutual Funds:

Liquid mutual funds are a class of mutual funds that hold short-term debt securities and hold a high liquidity with a relatively low risk. They are safer than equity mutual funds, but come with a greater rate of return than savings accounts. Liquid funds may be withdrawn, that is, redeemed, in a maximum of 24 hours, and hence are suitable as an emergency fund.

Money Market Funds:

Money market funds hold short-term, high quality debt instruments, including Treasury bills, certificates of deposit, and commercial paper. They provide higher yields than (for example) savings accounts and are of relatively low risk. These are extremely liquid and thus, are appropriate for an emergency fund. They however have a small degree of risk, therefore, it is important to evaluate if the risk profile is suitable before investing.

Government Bonds or Treasury Bills:

Government bonds (or treasury bills (T-bills) are low risk, debt securities backed by the government. Although, they provide safety, may have low returns in comparison with other investments. Short-term T-bills can be a tempting choice when you are looking for safety, but may not give you immediate access to funds as an account with banks or liquid mutual funds do.

Cash and Cash Equivalents:

If desired, absolute capital safety and instant access to your capital might be maintained by holding a portion of your emergency fund in cash or cash-like investments (i.e., short term government securities), that can easily be turned back into cash as needed.

Tips for Building and Maintaining Your Emergency Fund

Set a Clear Goal: Calculate which amount of money you would like to save, based on your monthly costs and cash situation. Break your goal into smaller milestones to make it more achievable and track your progress.

Automate Savings: Set up an automatic transfer from your main bank account to your emergency fund account each month. That provides you with a predictable way to make a fund contribution and it without the urge to part with the money.

Start Small, But Start Now: If you're unable to save the full amount immediately, don't be discouraged. Start with whatever amount you can afford and increase it gradually. Even a small emergency fund is better than none.

Replenish After Use: Use your emergency fund, if you do have to dip into it, first of all try and replenish it quickly. To stay on budget, make sure the fund is always fully stocked for the next crisis.

Review Regularly: Life changes, and so do your financial needs. Review your emergency fund annually to ensure it still meets your needs. For instance, if your salary increases, you have a family, or you take on more debt, you may need to build up your emergency fund more.

A financial cushion called an emergency fund is an integral component of budgeting, which acts as a buffer against unplanned financial setbacks. In cases of unforeseen costs, creating an emergency fund of 3 to 6 months' worth of household living expenses, and holding back investments in low risk, liquid assets such as savings accounts, fixed deposits or liquid mutual funds will see you through anything life throws at you. Get started on your emergency fund today, even if it is just a little, and build towards a more resilient financial future gradually.

Chapter 9: Goal-Based Investing: Achieving Your Financial Goals

Goal-based investing is a systematic way of organizing a portfolio by making the objective of the portfolio of financial goals. Rather than blindly investing for the purpose of accumulating capital, you make investments that are targeted to achieve a specific goal, for example, to finance the purchase of a house, retirement, financing your child's education or launching a business. In this approach, you can keep track of yourself, check the results and take more intelligent decisions, returning to your long-term goals. In this chapter, we'll discuss how to set clear, measurable financial goals, align your investment strategies to these goals, and adjust them as necessary to achieve success.

Why Goal-Based Investing Is Important

Provides Purpose and Direction:

Investing without a stated goal can be at times a difficult and discouraging process. Once you have a clear definition of your aim, you can focus your time and work on reaching it, and thus the act of investing becomes more meaningful and engaging. Since you have an idea of why you are saving money, you are more likely to stick with the plan, even when the market is unsettled.

Helps in Risk Management:

Various financial goals are accompanied by various time horizons and risk profiles. For instance, investing for a short-term objective (e.g., a trip or purchase of a car) involves lower risk than investing for long-term objectives (e.g., retirement). Goal-based investing enables you to adjust the risk of your investment according to its time frame to more carefully manage the risk associated with that investment.

Increases the Probability of Reaching Your Goals:

Research is clear that individuals setting out specific, measurable objectives are more likely to accomplish their objective. Goal-oriented investing has a defined target, a roadmap to it, and a means to track progress, making it more likely to produce a positive outcome.

Helps with Prioritization:

Goal-based investing enables you to give them priority when you have more than one financial target (e.g., buying a house, funding your child's education, and funding retirement). This guarantees that you will scale up and down resources effectively in a way that focuses most on the highest priority objective, or that which offers the greatest immediate benefit, before planning for long-term objectives.

Steps to Setting Clear, Measurable Financial Goals

Identify Your Goals:

Goal based investing commences with the establishment of financial objectives. These could include:

Short-term goals (0-3 years): E.g., saving for a house, buying a car or going on vacation.

Medium-term goals (3-10 years): Such as an down payment on a house or an educational fund for a child.
Long-term goals (10+ years): E.g., retirement savings, entrepreneuring, or a bequest).
Every goal needs a different investment strategy depending on how much time you have to accomplish it, as well as how much risk you are pleased to take.

Make Goals SMART:

To increase your chances of achieving your financial goals, make them SMART:

Specific: Define exactly what you want to achieve. E.g., "Save ₹20 lakhs for my child's advanced study" is more concrete than "Save for my child's education.

Measurable: You should be able to track progress. For example, if you want to save a sum of ₹20 lakhs, you can determine the amount of saving you need to do each month or year.

Achievable: Make sure your objectives are achievable (in light of your income, savings propensity, and time horizon).

Relevant: Select objectives that match your values and life priorities.

Time-bound: Set deadlines for achieving each goal. This helps keep you focused and motivated.

Estimate the Amount Needed for Each Goal:

For each objective, determine the sum of money required in order to meet the goal's deadline. For instance, if you are saving to buy a house, think about a houses current price, the percentage of price you have to put down, and other costs. Likewise, for retirement, estimate the annual amount of money that will be accessible to sustain your life-style in retirement, considering inflation and mortality.

Break Down Large Goals:

Large goals can be overwhelming, so break them into smaller, more manageable milestones. For example, if you want to save ₹1 crore for retirement, break it down into yearly or monthly savings targets to ensure you stay on track.

Aligning Investment Strategies with Your Goals

After identification and establishment of specific financial targets, the next step is to match investment strategies to each one of these targets. If the objectives are different, the method to be used will vary according to the time horizon and the risk tolerance.

Short-Term Goals (0-3 years): As short-term goals are also nearer in time, you should give preference to safety and liquidity. You certainly do not want to risk losing your money just as you need it. Investment options include:

i.   High-yield savings accounts

ii.   Liquid mutual funds

iii.   Fixed deposits (FDs) with a short maturity period

iv.   Government bonds (short-term) These are options that offer stability and easy fund access with some return.

Medium-Term Goals (3-10 years): In the medium-term vision, it is possible to accept a greater risk level because you have the possibility to recover from short-term market repulsions. Investment options include:

i.   Balanced mutual funds (equity-debt mix)

ii.   Index funds

iii.   Equity mutual funds (with a moderate risk profile)

iv.   Exchange-traded funds (ETFs)

These options offer higher returns compared to short-term options but still allow you to take a more cautious approach than with long-term investments.

Long-Term Goals (10+ years): For long-term objectives, for example, retirement, it is safe to have an exposure to more risk in return for possibly better outcomes. The higher time horizon allows your investments to weather market declines. Suitable options include:

i.   Equity mutual funds

ii.   Stocks

iii.   Retirement-focused funds (e.g., PPF, NPS in India)

iv.   Real estate investments

Target-date funds (for aged people's saving), In this type of investment, the values of the funds will grow enormously during a period of time and generate very large percentage of returns when compounding for years of time.

Adjusting Your Investment Strategy Over Time

Your investment strategies will need to evolve as your goals progress and life circumstances change. Here are some considerations for adjusting your strategy:

Review Regularly: Take the time to review your financial plan and investments at least once per year. It guarantees that you stay on the path to achieving your targets and that your investment approach continues to be consistent with any evolution in your financial status.

Rebalance Your Portfolio: The closer your goal is, the risk in your portfolio may become less desirable, which makes the analysis of risk in the bottom layer metrics even more complex. For instance, in the phase the comes with retirement, you may shift a greater part of your holdings to less risky, conservative holdings. On the other hand, if you are a long way from the target state, you may choose to elevate your exposure to riskier securities such as equities in order to achieve the highest level of returns.

Adapt to Life Changes: Life changing events, including marriage, procreation, career change, or relocation to a new town, can affect your financial aspirations. Be adaptive and modify your savings rate, investment strategy or even your objectives in response to these changes.

Stay Focused and Avoid Impulse Decisions: Although it is important to be adaptive, do not make fast moves on the market that are driven by fleeting short-term market movements or emotionally driven responses. Follow your plan and be flexible--adjust as needed around long-term objectives rather than short-term fluctuations.

Goal-based investing is a sophisticated method to fulfill your financial goals, by linking your investments to your personal goals. No matter you are saving for owning a house, for retirement or for your child's school, establish clear, quantifiable targets and formulate a plan to fit both of the targets' time span and their risk profile, it can improve the success rate a lot. Periodically check and update your plan and do not give up on your financial goals. Through purposeful investing, your dreams for financial security can be realized.

Chapter 10: Understanding Risk Appetite and Risk Tolerance

When it comes to investing, understanding your risk appetite and risk tolerance is crucial to making decisions that align with your financial goals and comfort level. Although risk is always present in any investment, how much risk you are often to take and how much risk you feel able to accept is different from person to person. This chapter explains the concept of risk appetite, how to assess your own risk tolerance, and how both factors influence the type of investments you should make.

What is Risk Appetite?

Risk appetite represents the amount of risk you are able to accept to gain your investment goals. It is an a priori subjective measure of your willingness to take a certain amount of risks, which is generally determined by your financial objectives, investment horizon, and/or your personality. Understanding your risk appetite helps determine the appropriate investment strategy, including how much exposure you should have to volatile assets like stocks or safer assets like bonds.

What is Risk Tolerance?

Risk tolerance is in contrast to the amount of risk you can actually afford to financially support. It is a function of your ability to cope with loss before it seriously impacts your financial security. However, risk appetite refers to amount risk you are prepared to incur while risk tolerance refers to

the amount of risk you are able to afford based on your financial situation.
In simple terms:

Risk Appetite: How much risk you are willing to take.

Risk Tolerance: How much risk you can afford to take.
Key Differences Between Risk Appetite and Risk Tolerance

Willingness vs. Ability:

Risk appetite is about your willingness to take on risk. It is affected by such variables as goals, personality traits, and psychological mechanisms.

Risk tolerance is about your ability to handle risk. It depends on your financial situation, such as income, assets, liabilities, and overall financial health.

Personal Factors:

Risk appetite can be a matter of more subjectiveness and of personality, and of personal taste. In addition, somebody who loves undertaking risks may be more likely to risk it all for the payoff of higher returns. Yet risk tolerance is ultimately determined more by tangible factors, such as income, savings, and existing debt.

Changing Over Time:

Risk appetite can evolve with personal situation, for example, a speedier accumulation of capital, or a more cautious attitude as one is approaching retirement. Risk tolerance, however, tends to be more stable over time, but it can also change in response to major life events like a significant change in income, family size, or retirement.

Assessing Your Own Risk Tolerance

In order to measure your own risk appetite, you have to weigh objective elements (your financial status) and subjective elements (your willingness to be uncertain). Here's a process for evaluating your risk tolerance:

Evaluate Your Financial Situation:

Income Stability: How stable is your income? If you have a stable, high income, you may be able to tolerate higher risks. When your income is variable or uncertain, may be preferable to adopt a more conservative one.

Expenses and Debts: Take into account your recurrent costs as well as large outstanding debts. Individuals having less financial burdens/liabilities tend to have higher risk tolerance since they are less directly dependent on their investments for short-term financial obligations.

Assets and Net Worth: If you have significant assets and a strong net worth, you might afford to take on more risk in your investment portfolio.

Emergency Fund: The presence of an emergency cushion enables an individual to take on more risk knowing he/she is not without resources to fall back on in case of market instability or financial crisis.

Assess Your Investment Horizon:

Short-Term vs. Long-Term Goals: If the financial objectives are short-term 1-3 years), a preeminence of safety is a worth consideration of return. However, if your goals are long-term (5+ years), you may be able to take on more risk with the potential for higher returns, as there's more time to recover from market fluctuations.

Goal Specifics: The urgency of the goal also matters. For example, if you're saving for a child's education in 2 years, your risk tolerance will likely be lower compared to someone investing for retirement 30 years down the line.

Understand Your Emotional Response to Risk:

Emotional Comfort: How would you feel if the value of your investments dropped by 10%, 20%, or more? Are you comfortable with fluctuations in your portfolio, or do you panic at the thought of losses? Your affective response to risk may be a dependable measure of actual risk appetite.

Previous Experiences: Past experiences in investing, such as whether you've experienced a significant market downturn, can provide insight into your comfort level with volatility.

Risk Tolerance Questionnaire:

A great number of financial institutions and investment platforms offer risk tolerance questionnaires. These are valuable instruments which measure, for instance, your target financial goals, horizon of your investments and emotional response to market uncertainty to uniquely identify your risk tolerance. Answers to these questionnaires usually categorize you as a conservative, balanced or aggressive investor.

Types of Risk Tolerance Profiles

Conservative Risk Tolerance:

Profile: Investors with a conservative risk tolerance prioritize the safety of their principal investment. They are risk-shy and want secure/predictable returns and low loss.

Investment Strategy: Conservative investors also tend to put a large chunk of their portfolio in low-risk assets e.g., bonds, money market funds, or other fixed-income securities. They may also have cash reserves to ensure liquidity.

deal for: People in pre-retirement age, people with short-term financial needs, or people with low resistance to risk (e.g., inexperienced, risk-averse).

Moderate Risk Tolerance:

Profile: Moderate investors are not afraid of a little greater risk in the prospect of a much greater reward. Nevertheless, they also still favor risk/safety balance.

Investment Strategy: A relatively balanced portfolio usually consists of a portfolio of stocks and bonds, with part dedicated to growth stocks and part dedicated to fixed-income securities to yield stability.

Ideal for: People with a medium to long-term time horizon and some degree of financial buffer.

Aggressive Risk Tolerance:

Profile: Investors who are happy to tolerate relatively high levels of risk are willing to accept a rather high level of risk in order to attain a very high level of return. They are unfazed by the chance of volatility and short-term loss.

Investment Strategy: Aggressive investors generally exposure a significant part of their portfolio to equities, such as individual stocks and growth-oriented mutual funds or exchange-traded funds (ETFs). They may also consider emerging markets or alternative investments.

Ideal for: Retail investors with long-term objectives (e.g., retirement savings), or financially well-situated investors to withstand short-term market volatility.

How Risk Appetite and Tolerance Influence Investment Decisions

Understanding your risk appetite and tolerance helps you make informed decisions about the types of investments that align with your financial goals. Here's how they influence your investment choices:

Asset Allocation:

Your risk tolerance will help determine the appropriate asset allocation (the mix of stocks, bonds, real estate, and other assets) for your portfolio. For example:

Unlike less conservative investors, conservative investors will hold a higher percentage of bonds and cash-equivalents in their portfolio.

Moderate investors will have a mix of stocks and bonds.

Aggressive investors will pay a higher proportion to equities, aiming at greater growth in the long term.

Choice of Investments:

Risk appetite and tolerance dictates the type of investment you select. For example:

In case you are of low risk tolerance, you may not buy risky stocks, but you may rather to invest in government bonds or index funds.

For those who are susceptible to heightened risk, individual stocks or sector-focused funds could be chosen over other growth options.

Rebalancing and Monitoring:

Over time, market movements can affect your risk profile. Rebalancing your portfolio to match your evolving risk tolerance—most notably as you approach or reach your financial goals and as life events occur—is, and must be, part of the financial plan.

Understanding your risk appetite and risk tolerance is essential for successful investing. Risk appetite is the degree of risk which you are prepared to accept in order to achieve your goals, whereas risk tolerance reflects the amount of risk you are able to readily sustain financially. Through also ratings of these issues, it is possible to make informed choices about asset allocation and to select investments that fit your comfort level and financial ability. Remember, risk tolerance is not static—it can evolve over time, so it's important to periodically reassess it and adjust your investment strategies accordingly.

Chapter 11: Alternative Investment Options in India

Beyond more classical investment products, such as stocks, bonds, and fixed deposits, alternative investments open doors to portfolio diversification and can yield good returns. Although these alternative investments have the potential to improve portfolio performance, they have their own special risks and complexities. This chapter explores some popular alternative investment options available in India, including real estate, gold, stocks, peer-to-peer lending, cryptocurrencies, and commodities trading, and provides insight into how they can be used to diversify and grow your investments.

1. Real Estate

Real estate has long been a popular alternative investment option in India. It allows for the possibility of both capital appreciation and rental income, making it an attractive option for investors looking for long-term growth.

Types of Real Estate Investments:

Residential Properties: Buying homes or apartments for resale or rental income.

Commercial Properties: Real estate financing (office, retail, or industrial properties), in anticipation of either rental income or capital gains.

Real Estate Investment Trusts (REITs): A more liquid alternative to direct real estate investment. REITs gather

capital with which to invest in a set of real estate assets, and to pay out the profits to the investors.
Benefits:

Tangible asset with potential for steady cash flow.

Long-term appreciation due to urbanization and infrastructure growth.

Diversification out of mainstream markets, such as equities and bonds.

Risks:

High initial costs and inaccessibility (difficulty to sell quickly).

Market movement and regional economic climate impacting property values.

For example, Regulatory risks (i.e., alteration of regulatory frameworks governing land use or government policies).

2. Gold

Gold is a safe-haven asset for centuries and is also one of the most favored alternative assets in India. It is a protection against both inflation and economic uncertainty.

Types of Gold Investments:

Physical Gold: Jewellery, gold coins, and bars. However, physical gold requires storage and security.

Gold ETFs (Exchange-Traded Funds): A more liquid option, gold ETFs track the price of gold and can be bought and sold on stock exchanges.

Benefits:

Forms the hedge against inflation and devaluation of currencies.

High liquidity, especially through ETFs.
Historically strong long-term returns.

Risks:

No income generation (like interest or dividends).

Price volatility influenced by global gold prices.

Storage and insurance costs for physical gold.

3. Stocks (Equities)

Equities are one of the most common forms of alternative investment, providing investors with an opportunity to invest in the ownership of companies and potentially earn returns through price appreciation and dividends.

Types of Stock Investments:

Direct Stocks: Holding companies publicly traded on stock exchanges (such as the Bombay Stock Exchange (BSE) and the National Stock Exchange (NSE).

Equity Mutual Funds: Pooled investments in a portfolio of stocks, managed by fund managers. They offer diversification and professional management.

Index Funds: A passive form of equity investing that tracks a market index like the Nifty 50 or Sensex.
Benefits:

High potential for capital appreciation and dividends.

Liquidity, as stocks are easily traded on exchanges.

Potential for significant returns, particularly in high-growth sectors.
Risks:

Market volatility and price fluctuations.

Specific to the company such as management changes, financial condition, or competitive market conditions.

Requires time and research to select individual stocks.

4. Peer-to-Peer (P2P) Lending

P2P lending facilitates the direct lending of money from one person to another through internet platforms, outside of traditional banks and financial intermediaries. It offers investors an opportunity to earn a return on capital at the same time it enables people or companies to obtain a loan.

How It Works:

Investors lend money to borrowers through a P2P lending platform).

In exchange, the investors are given interest accrued on the loan base term.

Surcharges are usually made and the lending process is mediated, guaranteeing creditworthiness for the borrower.
Benefits:

Potential for high returns, often with interest rates exceeding interest rates from traditional fixed-income investments.

Direct access to the lending market without intermediaries.

Diversification into a different asset class.

Risks:

Borrower defaults could lead to loss of principal.

Different platforms have different levels of due diligence and risk mitigation.

Regulatory ambiguity in the P2P lending market in India.

5. Cryptocurrencies

Cryptocurrencies, such as Bitcoin, Ethereum, and others are digital assets that, for their decentralized transactions, are based on blockchain technology. Cryptocurrencies have been attractive as an alternative investment class but they carry very high volatility.

Types of Cryptocurrency Investments:

Bitcoin and Ethereum: The two most well-known and widely used cryptocurrencies.

Altcoins: Other cryptocurrencies like Ripple (XRP), Litecoin, and more.

Cryptocurrency Funds: Mutual funds or ETFs that invest in a portfolio of cryptocurrencies, granting exposure across a portfolio of digital assets.

Benefits:

High potential returns due to rapid price movements.

Provides a hedge against currency depreciation and economic turmoil.

Decentralized and accessible worldwide.

Risks:

Extreme volatility and price fluctuations.

Regulatory risks, because cryptocurrencies are being investigated in a global regulatory way by the governments of numerous countries.

Vulnerabilities to hacking or theft from digital wallets.

6. Commodities Trading

Commodities trading is the trading of physical assets, namely crude oil and natural gas as well as food stuffs (grain, cotton, sugar), and metals. Investors can participate in commodities trading through direct investment in the physical asset or via commodity futures contracts.

Types of Commodities:

Precious Metals: Gold, silver, platinum.

Energy: Oil, natural gas.
Agricultural Products: Wheat, coffee, cotton.

Base Metals: Copper, aluminum.

Benefits:

Provides diversification away from traditional financial markets.

Acts as a hedge against inflation, especially in the case of precious metals.

High liquidity in certain commodities markets.

Risks:

Price fluctuations driven by global supply-demand, meteorological, geopolitical, and macroeconomic factors.

    i.   Requires specialized knowledge and research.
   ii.   Commodities futures may contain high leverage and the risk of margin calls.

Alternative investment options in India, such as real estate, gold, stocks, peer-to-peer lending, cryptocurrencies, and commodities, can serve as valuable tools for diversifying your investment portfolio. All of these are in their own right with pros and cons, and it is important to know how each investment works before putting your investors' capital into it.

Diversification should be a primary consideration when using alternative investments, as the latter can minimize risk and deliver higher returns in niche market situations.

The risk appetite, the investment horizon, and the financial goals one is trying to achieve must be considered when making alternative investments.

Advice from professionals and thorough research are important, and even more so when facing higher-risk options such as cryptocurrency or commodities.

By broadening the range of investment choices available to you to include alternatives, it may be possible to achieve higher overall returns, hedge against inflation, and construct a more robust portfolio.

Chapter 12: Financial Planning and Budgeting

Financial planning is an important first step to gaining control over your finances. It gives you a sense of where the money actually goes, allows you to always have a financial plan for future plans, and can help you to manage your resources well. Whether you're planning for short-term expenses or long-term goals like retirement or your children's education, having a clear financial plan and budget in place is essential. The current section describes the foundation required for the design of budgets, debt management, tax planning and saving for major events of life.

Creating a Budget

A budget is a guide that allows you to monitor your income and spending in an effort to live financially sound and to save for the future. Creating a budget involves the following steps:

Assess Your Income: Start by calculating all your sources of income. This includes earned income, business income, rent income, etc. Understanding your total monthly income is the first step toward effective budgeting.

Track Your Expenses: Record all your monthly expenses. They are, for example, fixed expenditure (rent, utilities, insurance premiums) and marginal expenditure (groceries, entertainment, and carrying out of meals in restaurants). Be honest and thorough to get an accurate picture.

Set Financial Goals: Identify your financial goals. These could range from saving for an emergency fund to buying a home, going on a vacation, or saving for retirement. Your goals will help prioritize your spending and savings.

Create a Spending Plan: Assign fixed budgetary amounts to each category in accordance with your needs. The concept is to make sure that you are not spending more than you earn and keeping money aside for saving.

The 50/30/20 Rule: A popular rule of thumb for personal budgeting is the 50/30/20 rule:

50% of your earnings are spent on needs (rent, utilities, insurance, etc.).

30% is devoted to wants (leisure, eating out, traveling, etc.).

20% goes toward savings and debt repayment.

Monitor and Adjust: Budgets should be reviewed on a regular basis and spending tracked in order to stay within budget. Adjust your budget, if necessary, especially when there are changes in your income or expenses.

Managing Debt

Debt management is a critical aspect of financial planning. Properly managing debt ensures that you don't overwhelm yourself with financial obligations while still working toward your goals.

Identify and Prioritize Debt: Make a list of all your debts, including loans, credit card balances, and any outstanding payments. Consciously first make high-interest debt payments (e.g., credit card debt) in order to prevent accruing that high-interest payment.

Create a Debt Repayment Plan: Consider methods like the Debt Snowball (paying off the smallest debts first to build momentum) or Debt Avalanche (paying off the highest-interest debts first to minimize interest payments). Choose the method that fits your situation.

Refinancing and Consolidation: When you have a number of high-interest debt you should consolidate them into one new loan, lower interest rate, or refinance your existing loans with lower monthly payments.

Avoid Taking on Unnecessary Debt: Limit borrowing to what is necessary, and ensure that you can comfortably meet monthly repayment obligations. Credit cards should be used wisely, and a consumer should not obtain credit card debt for non-necessary items.

Build Creditworthiness: Responsible management of debt improves your credit score, making it easier to get better loan terms and interest rates in the future. Always make timely payments and avoid maxing out credit limits.

Tax Planning

Intelligent tax planning not only saves you money but also guarantees that you stay compliant with tax regulations. In India, tax planning should be a part of your overall financial strategy to keep more of your income for savings and investments.

Understand Your Taxable Income: Your taxable income is the amount of income that you need to pay taxes on, after deductions for allowances, exemptions and rebates. It's essential to know how much you are earning and what portion is taxable.

Maximize Deductions and Exemptions:

Section 80C: Under this segment, the taxpayer is eligible to take deductions up to ₹1.5 lakh for investments in certain financial products like Life Insurance premium, PPF (Public Provident Fund), ELSS (Equity-linked Savings Schemes), and NPS (National Pension Scheme).

Section 80D: Deductions on premiums paid for health insurance policies for yourself, your spouse, children, and parents.

Section 24(b): Deductions on home loan interest (upto ₹2 lakh per annum for self-utilized property).

Invest in Tax-Advantaged Accounts: Use investment instruments that offer tax benefits, such as the PPF, NPS, and tax-saving fixed deposits. These investments not only help you save on taxes but also build long-term wealth.

Plan for Capital Gains Tax: Understand the tax implications of your investments, especially when selling assets like stocks, mutual funds, or real estate. Long-term capital gains

(LTCG) bear a lower rate than short-term capital gains (STCG), so below one should retain the assets for a period in mind to minimize tax liability.

Tax-Saving Investments: Use tax-saving instruments, like NPS, PPF, or ELSS, to lower your taxable income and create retirement wealth.

Saving for Major Life Goals

Financial planning is used to make certain that you have the available funds to reach life's major achievements, like buying a house, paying for your children to go to school, or to prepare for pension.

Retirement Planning:

Start saving early for retirement to take advantage of compounding. Maintain a regular contribution to retirement-oriented accounts, such as the National Pension System (NPS), Employee Provident Fund (EPF), or others long-term investment instruments.

Employ retirement calculators in order to estimate the kind and magnitude of money you will need at retirement, and so invest accordingly in assets capable of appreciation, such as mutual funds, shares or real estate.

Education Planning for Children:

Begin saving for your children's education early to benefit from the power of compounding.

Thinks about Sukanya Samriddhi Yojana (SSY) as applicable to his/her daughters or education-oriented mutual funds, as well as fixed deposits, offering attractive long-term return.

Emergency Fund:

An emergency fund should be a priority in your financial plan. Attempt to preserve at least 3-6 months of living expenses in an easily accessible, low-risk holding, including savings account, short-term fixed deposits, or money market fund.

Buying a Home:

Begin saving for a home down payment early. It may also be worth building an account specifically for savings (e.g. or investing in a fixed investment plan (e.g., SIP), aimed at long term growth.

Health Planning:

Save yourself and family from financial losses due to medical bills by getting health insurance. Be sure that the protection is sufficient for your family and that premiums are taken into consideration while creating your monthly budget.

Review and Adjust Your Financial Plan

Financial planning is not a one-time activity, it is an ongoing activity. Life circumstances change—whether it's a job change, marriage, children, or retirement—and your financial plan must adapt accordingly.

Monitor Progress: Regularly review your budget, debt repayment plan, and investment portfolio to ensure that you're on track to meet your goals.

Adjust for Life Changes: When life events occur, e.g., salary increase, marriage, child finishing school, revise your financial plans and objectives to account for new priorities.

Seek Professional Advice: It is suggested to work with a financial planner together to give investment advice, tax planning and overall planning about investments.

Financial planning and budgeting are critical to long-term financial stability and success. If you build a strong budget, manage down debt, plan for taxes and prepare for big life aspirations, you are in the driver's seat of your finances. Do it early, be disciplined, and periodically review your plan to account for all changes. With careful financial planning, you can not only achieve your goals but also build a strong foundation for your financial well-being.

Chapter 13: Conclusion

In this last chapter we review the fundamentals of an individual's personal financial management as well as highlight the necessity of financial control for the attainment of long-term financial health. No matter if you are just beginning a journey in finance or trying to optimize your current plan, all the insights and assets discussed all through this book are the next step in the direction of financial independence and/or security.

Key Principles of Personal Finance

Financial Planning and Budgeting: To successfully manage money, maintaining a transparent financial plan is the basis. Making a budget, keeping track of expenditures and making financial goals keeps you on track and makes sure the money you have is in synch with your long-term aspirations.

Investing for the Future: Investing is a key component of building wealth. Whether it's through stocks, mutual funds, bonds, or alternative assets, understanding the different investment options and how to diversify your portfolio allows you to take advantage of compounding and grow your wealth over time.

Managing Debt: Effective debt management is crucial to maintaining financial stability. Financial control, along with the high costs associated with financial exposure, is achievable through direct effort such as preventing excessive debt, focusing on high-interest liabilities, and developing a repayment strategy.

Risk Management: Protecting yourself, your family, and your assets through insurance is a critical aspect of financial planning. Health insurance, life insurance, and property insurance safeguard against unforeseen financial challenges.

Tax Planning and Saving: Knowledge of tax legislation and utilization of deductions, exemptions, and tax-saving investments enable us to reduce tax obligations with greater freedom to save and invest.

Emergency Fund: Emergency fund accumulation is a form of financial safety net for unforeseen events, so that you never have to fall back on debt.

The Importance of Financial Discipline

Financial discipline is the cornerstone of achieving your goals. It demands ongoing work, thoughtful decision-making and a willingness to live within limits. If you learn good habits, like consistently saving, refraining from impulsive purchases, and consistently learning about money management, then you can create a strong base for financial mastery.

Some ways to maintain financial discipline include:

Periodically reviewing your budget and making changes in the case of updates in income or expenses.

Maintaining a long-term perspective on your financial goals even when deciding to make short-term spending choices.

Continuously learning about new investment opportunities, tax laws, and financial products to make informed decisions.

Continued Education in Financial Literacy

Financial literacy is a lifelong journey. Knowledge must not get static in this dynamic market, tax legislation, and investment process. Keeping up with financial knowledge regularly equip you to make more effective decisions, stay away from traps, and grab opportunities that arise.

Stay Informed: Read books, sign up for courses, go to seminars and participate in discussion with financial professionals to expand your knowledge.

Seek Professional Advice: Seek the advice of financial planners, tax preparers, and investors so that your strategy is as efficient as possible and meets your needs.

Adapt to Change: As your life circumstances change (e.g., marriage, children, retirement), continuously revisit and revise your financial plan to stay on track.

Achieving Financial Independence and Security

Personal finance ends up with people's ultimate goal to financial independence and security. By applying the principles outlined in this book, you can work toward creating a life where money is a tool that works for you, rather than something you work for. Financial independence means having the freedom to make decisions based on your values and goals, without being constrained by financial worries.

Set Clear Financial Goals: From buying a house to retirement savings or college fundings, knowing exactly where you want to go helps you to concentrate and stay motivated.

Be Patient and Consistent: Wealth accumulation does not happen overnight, but if you stay disciplined, make good choices and keep at it, you'll be well on your way to financial independence.

Prioritize Your Well-Being: Financial security is not only about building fortunes; it is a balance. Don't forget to enjoy life, focus on health, and maintain meaningful relationships while working toward your financial goals.

Final Thoughts

In conclusion, the path to financial independence and security begins with education, planning, and discipline. The principles and strategies that are the subject of this book provide an integrative guide to your financial course of action. Remember that financial wealth is not acquired in a day, but as a result of a consistent process of learning, thoughtful management, and planned investments, it is possible to achieve a stable and flourishing future.

If you would proactively, act today, you are putting ourselves in position to achieve a financially free tomorrow. Stay disciplined, keep learning, and always stay focused on your long-term goals. Your financial future is your power—take charge and make the life you deserve.

Author Biography

Arif Mohamed is a highly experienced and passionate Personal Finance Coach, with over two decades of expertise in guiding individuals toward financial empowerment.

With over 2 decades of experience in personal finance management, Arif has worked with a diverse range of individuals—from young professionals taking their first steps into financial planning to seasoned investors looking to refine their strategies. Throughout these years, Arif has honed a deep understanding of the intricacies of investments, budgeting, tax planning, and wealth creation, providing personalized solutions that reflect the financial landscape of India.

Because financial literacy is lacking for a large number of adults, Arif has dedicated himself to educating and enabling as many as possible. To date, he has trained over 20,000 individuals through interactive seminars and workshops, equipping them with practice al tools to manage their finances effectively and make informed investment choices. Through these sessions, Arif has built a reputation for being approachable, insightful, and dedicated to helping people understand and take control of their financial futures.

Simplicity forms the basis for Arif's personal finance education strategy, to demystify financial notions into easily comprehended principles. As a coach, he emphasizes goal-based investing, strategic money management, and the power of compounding to ensure that financial freedom is accessible to everyone, regardless of their background.

Through this book, Arif hopes to inspire and equip readers to take control of their financial journeys, understand the importance of smart money management, and ultimately achieve financial independence.

www.ingramcontent.com/pod-product-compliance
Lightning Source LLC
Chambersburg PA
CBHW061435160726

47995CB00003B/907